I Like Biographies! Bilingual

Lee sobre
Sacagawea
Read About Sacagawea

Stephen Feinstein

Enslow Elementary
an imprint of
Enslow Publishers, Inc.

40 Industrial Road   PO Box 38
Box 398   Aldershot
Berkeley Heights, NJ 07922   Hants GU12 6BP
USA   UK
http://www.enslow.com

Words to Know

explorer—A person who travels into new lands.

Minnetaree (Mih-neh-TA-ree)— An Indian tribe that lived along the Missouri River in North Dakota.

moccasin—A soft slipper made of leather.

Shoshone (Sho-SHO-nee)— An Indian tribe that lived on both sides of the Rocky Mountains.

Palabras a conocer

el explorador—Una persona que viaja a nuevas tierras.

los minitari—Una tribu india que vivía a lo largo del Río Missouri en el estado de Dakota del Norte.

el mocasín—Calzado blando hecho de cuero.

los shoshone—Una tribu india que vivía en las laderas de las Montañas Rocosas.

Enslow Elementary, an imprint of Enslow Publishers, Inc. Enslow Elementary® is a registered trademark of Enslow Publishers, Inc.

Bilingual edition copyright © 2006 by Enslow Publishers, Inc. Originally published in English under the title *Read About Sacagawea* © 2004 by Enslow Publishers, Inc. Bilingual edition translated by Romina C. Cinquemani, edited by Susana C. Schultz, of Strictly Spanish, LLC.

Library of Congress Cataloging-in-Publication Data

Feinstein, Stephen.
[Read about Sacagawea. Spanish & English]
Lee sobre Sacagawea = Read about Sacagawea / Stephen Feinstein.— Bilingual ed.
p. cm. — (I like biographies! bilingual)
Includes bibliographical references and index.
ISBN 0-7660-2674-4
1. Sacagawea—Juvenile literature. 2. Lewis and Clark Expedition (1804–1806)—Juvenile literature. 3. Shoshoni women—Biography—Juvenile literature. 4. Shoshoni Indians—Biography—Juvenile literature. I. Title: Read about Sacagawea. II. Title. III. Series.
F592.7.S123F4518 2006
978.004'974574'0092—dc22
2005020387

Printed in the United States of America

10 9 8 7 6 5 4 3 2 1

To Our Readers: We have done our best to make sure all Internet addresses in this book were active and appropriate when we went to press. However, the author and the publishers have no control over and assume no liability for the material available on those Internet sites or on other Web sites they may link to. Any comments or suggestions can be sent by e-mail to comments@enslow.com or to the address on the back cover.

Every effort has been made to locate all copyright holders of material used in this book. If any errors or omissions have occurred, corrections will be made in future editions of this book.

Illustration Credits: AP/Wide World, p. 21; © Artville, LLC, p. 11; Denver Public Library, Western History Collection, call no. X33784, p. 1; Drawing by George Henry in Sacajawea, by Harold P. Howard. Published by the University of Oklahoma Press, Norman, 1971, p. 17; Library of Congress, p. 5; Edgar S. Paxson, "Sacagawea," oil on canvas, 1904, permanent collection The Montana Museum of Art and Culture, The University of Montana, p. 7; Courtesy Frederic Remington Art Museum, Ogdensburg, New York, p. 19; Charles M. Russell, "Lewis and Clark on the Lower Columbia," 1905, watercolor, 1961.195, © Amon Carter Museum, Fort Worth, Tex., p. 13; Charles M. Russell, "Lewis and Clark Expedition." From the collection of the Gilcrease Museum, Tulsa, Okla., p. 15; State Historical Society of North Dakota 85.22, p. 9; United States Mint, p. 3.

Cover Illustration: Painting by Carl Feryok.

Contents / Contenido

1

Growing Up in an Indian Village

Sacagawea was born in 1788. Her tribe of Shoshone Indians lived in the Rocky Mountains. When she was eleven, Sacagawea was captured by the Minnetaree Indians during a raid. They took Sacagawea to their village far to the east on the Great Plains.

Crecer en un pueblo indio

Sacagawea nació en 1788. Su tribu de indios shoshone vivía en las Montañas Rocosas. A los once años, Sacagawea fue capturada por los indios minitari durante una invasión. Ellos se llevaron a Sacagawea a su pueblo al este de las Grandes Planicies.

The Shoshone lived in tepees like these.

Los shoshone vivían en tipis como éstos.

Sacagawea grew into a strong young woman. She worked hard, helping the Minnetaree women grow corn, beans, and squash. The Minnetaree called her Bird Woman, a sign of respect. Sacagawea wished that she could fly like a bird. Then she would be able to fly home.

Sacagawea creció y se convirtió en una joven fuerte. Ella trabajaba duro y ayudaba a las mujeres minitari a cultivar maíz, frijoles y calabacines. Los minitari la llamaban Mujer Pájaro, como signo de respeto. Sacagawea deseaba poder volar como un pájaro. Así ella podría volar y regresar a su hogar.

There are no photographs of Sacagawea. This is what one artist thought she might have looked like.

No hay fotografías de Sacagawea. Así es como un artista pensó que ella pudo haberse visto.

2

— Sacagawea Meets Lewis and Clark —

In 1804, Sacagawea was sixteen. She was now married to a French Canadian fur trapper named Toussaint Charbonneau. One day, a group of forty white men traveled up the Missouri River in three boats. They were led by the explorers Meriwether Lewis and William Clark.

— Sacagawea conoce a Lewis y Clark —

En 1804, Sacagawea tenía dieciséis años. Ahora ella estaba casada con un canadiense francés llamado Toussaint Charbonneau que comerciaba en pieles de animales. Un día, un grupo de cuarenta hombres blancos viajaban por el Río Missouri en tres botes. A ellos los guiaban los exploradores Meriwether Lewis y William Clark.

This shows the first meeting between the explorers and Sacagawea. Behind them are the round earth houses of the Minnetaree.

Esto muestra el primer encuentro entre los exploradores y Sacagawea. Detrás de ellos están las viviendas redondas hechas de tierra de los minitari.

They had been sent by President Thomas Jefferson to explore the lands west of the Missouri River. They were looking for somebody who could speak to the Indians they would meet. They asked Sacagawea to come along to speak with the Shoshone. She could hardly believe her good luck! She would finally be going home.

Los había enviado el Presidente Thomas Jefferson a explorar las tierras al oeste del Río Missouri. Ellos estaban buscando a alguna persona que pudiera hablarle a los indios con los que podrían encontrarse. Ellos le pidieron a Sacagawea que los acompañara para hablar con los shoshone. ¡Ella apenas podía creer su buena suerte! Ella por fin volvería a su hogar.

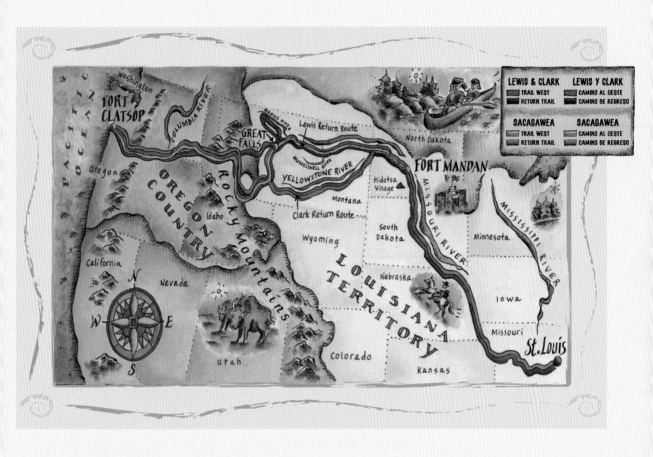

This map shows the route that the explorers took across America, from St. Louis to the Pacific Ocean.

Este mapa muestra la ruta que los exploradores tomaron a lo largo del territorio norteamericano, desde St. Louis hasta el Océano Pacífico.

3

Sacagawea Travels West

In April 1805, Lewis and Clark and their men set out across the plains. Charbonneau and Sacagawea walked with them. Sacagawea carried her two-month-old son, Pomp, on her back.

Sacagawea helped find food for the group. She gathered wood for the campfire. She even made moccasins for the men.

Sacagawea viaja al oeste

En abril de 1805, Lewis, Clark y sus hombres emprendieron su camino por las planicies. Charbonneau y Sacagawea caminaban con ellos. Sacagawea llevaba a su hijo de dos meses, Pomp, colgado de su espalda.

Sacagawea ayudaba a buscar alimentos para el grupo. Ella recolectaba madera para la fogata. Ella también hacía mocasines para los hombres.

Sacagawea helped Lewis and Clark in many ways. She spoke with other Indians and told them the explorers were friendly.

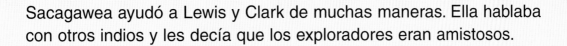

Sacagawea ayudó a Lewis y Clark de muchas maneras. Ella hablaba con otros indios y les decía que los exploradores eran amistosos.

After traveling through the Rocky Mountains, the explorers met a group of Shoshone Indians. Suddenly Sacagawea's eyes filled with tears of happiness. One of the Indians was her brother, Cameauhwait! She had not seen him since they were children. Now he was a chief. Sacagawea threw her arms around him.

Después de viajar a través de las Montañas Rocosas, los exploradores encontraron un grupo de indios shoshone. De pronto, los ojos de Sacagawea se llenaron con lágrimas de felicidad. ¡Uno de los indios era su hermano, Cameauhwait! Ella no lo había visto desde que eran niños. Ahora él era un jefe. Sacagawea lo abrazó.

Sacagawea was very happy when they met the Shoshone. In this painting, she is hugging a friend from her childhood.

Sacagawea estaba muy feliz cuando se encontraron con los shoshone. En esta pintura, ella está abrazando a una amiga de su infancia.

4

Sacagawea Sees the "Great Waters"

Sacagawea knew that Lewis and Clark wanted to go all the way to the "great waters." This was her name for the Pacific Ocean. Sacagawea hoped to see the "great waters," too. Her brother said he would help the explorers. He gave them horses for the trip.

Sacagawea ve las "grandes aguas"

Sacagawea sabía que Lewis y Clark querían ir hasta las "grandes aguas". Éste era el nombre que ella le daba al Océano Pacífico. Sacagawea también esperaba ver las "grandes aguas". Su hermano dijo que él ayudaría a los exploradores. Él les dio caballos para el viaje.

Sacagawea helped the explorers get horses from the Shoshone. Here she is riding with Pomp on her back.

Sacagawea ayudó a los exploradores a obtener caballos de los shoshone. Aquí está ella a caballo con Pomp en su espalda.

17

Once again the group traveled west. When they reached the Columbia River, they built canoes. They then traveled down the Columbia all the way to the Pacific Ocean. On November 15, 1805, Sacagawea stood on the beach. She could not take her eyes off the huge waves of the "great waters."

Otra vez, el grupo viajó hacia el oeste. Cuando llegaron al Río Columbia, ellos hicieron canoas. Luego ellos viajaron por el Columbia hasta llegar al Océano Pacífico. El 15 de noviembre de 1805, Sacagawea estaba en la playa. Ella no podía quitar la vista de las olas gigantes de las "grandes aguas".

This painting shows Lewis and Clark with Sacagawea and Charbonneau standing behind them. They are all in front of the Columbia River, which leads to the Pacific Ocean.

Esta pintura muestra a Lewis y Clark con Sacagawea y Charbonneau detrás de ellos. Todos están frente al Río Columbia, que desemboca en el Océano Pacífico.

HURON PUBLIC LIBRARY
521 DAKOTA AVE S
HURON, SD 57350

Sacagawea spent the winter on the beach with the explorers. She then traveled with them back to the Indian village on the Missouri River.

The brave Bird Woman died in December 1812. Lewis and Clark could not have made their trip without the help of Sacagawea.

Sacagawea pasó el invierno en la playa con los exploradores. Luego, ella regresó con ellos al pueblo indio en el Río Missouri.

La valiente Mujer Pájaro murió en diciembre de 1812. Lewis y Clark no podrían haber hecho su viaje sin la ayuda de Sacagawea.

There are many statues honoring Sacagawea. This one is in Portland, Oregon.

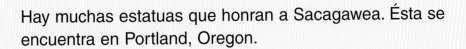

Hay muchas estatuas que honran a Sacagawea. Ésta se encuentra en Portland, Oregon.

Timeline

1788—Sacagawea is born to the Shoshone tribe.

About 1798—Sacagawea is captured by the Minnetaree Indians.

1804—Lewis and Clark begin their trip to explore the lands west of the Missouri River. Sacagawea joins them.

February 1805—Pomp is born.

August 1805—Sacagawea meets the Shoshone Indians again.

November 1805—The explorers reach the Pacific Ocean.

1806—The explorers travel back east. Sacagawea returns to the Minnetaree.

1812—Sacagawea dies in South Dakota.

Línea del tiempo

1788—Sacagawea nace en la tribu shoshone.

Alrededor de 1798—Sacagawea es capturada por los minitari.

1804—Lewis y Clark comienzan su viaje para explorar las tierras al oeste del Río Missouri. Sacagawea se une a ellos.

Febrero de 1805—Nace Pomp.

Agosto de 1805—Sacagawea se encuentra con los shoshone otra vez.

Noviembre de 1805—Los exploradores llegan al Océano Pacífico.

1806—Los exploradores viajan de regreso al este. Sacagawea regresa a los minitari.

1812—Sacagawea muere en Dakota del Sur.

Learn More/Más para aprender

Books/Libros

In English/En inglés

Adler, David A. *A Picture Book of Sacagawea*. New York: Holiday House, 2000.

Devillier, Christy. *Lewis & Clark*. Edina, Minn.: Abdo Publishing, 2001.

Milton, Joyce. *Sacajawea: Her True Story*. New York: Grosset & Dunlap, 2001.

Redmond, Shirley-Raye. *Lewis and Clark: A Prairie Dog for the President*. New York: Random House, 2003.

Internet Addresses/Direcciones de Internet

In English/En inglés

Lewis and Clark Journey of Discovery
<http://www.nps.gov/jeff/LewisClark2/HomePage/HomePage.htm>

National Geographic Kids, "Go West Across America with Lewis & Clark"
<http://nationalgeographic.com/west>

Index

Índice